Testimonials In Favour Of Alexander W. Robertson ...
Candidate For The Office Of Librarian Of The
Public Library Of The Burgh Of Aberdeen...

Anonymous

TESTIMONIALS

IN FAVOUR OF

ALEXANDER W. ROBERTSON, M.A.,

CANDIDATE

FOR THE

OFFICE OF LIBRARIAN OF THE PUBLIC LIBRARY

OF THE

BURGH OF ABERDEEN.

ABERDEEN UNIVERSITY PRESS.

CONTENTS.

———◦———

	PAGE
APPLICATION, ...	5

TESTIMONIALS from—

JOHN WEBSTER, LL.D., M.P. for the City of Aberdeen,	9
Sir WILLIAM FORBES, Bart. of Craigievar, . . .	11
Sir JOHN ANDERSON, LL.D., ...	13
JOHN F. WHITE, M.A., Merchant in Aberdeen, . .	15
WM. D. GEDDES, M.A., LL.D., Professor of Greek, University of Aberdeen, ...	17
Rev. WM. MILLIGAN, M.A., D.D., Professor of Divinity and Biblical Criticism, University of Aberdeen, .	19
Rev. JOHN FYFE, M.A., Professor of Moral Philosophy, University of Aberdeen, ...	21
WM. STIRLING, M.D., Sc.D., Professor of Institutes of Medicine, University of Aberdeen, . . .	23
JAMES W. H. TRAIL, M.A., M.D., Professor of Botany, University of Aberdeen, ...	25
ALEX. DYCE DAVIDSON, M.A., M.D., Professor of Materia Medica, University of Aberdeen, . .	27
WM. MINTO, M.A., Professor of Logic and English Language and Composition, University of Aberdeen, ...	29
ALEX. OGSTON, M.A., M.D., Professor of Surgery, University of Aberdeen, ...	31
ROBERT WALKER, M.A., F.R.S.E., Librarian to the University of Aberdeen, ...	33

TESTIMONIALS from—

PAGE

RICHARD GARNETT, LL.D., Superintendent of the
Reading Room of the British Museum, . . 37

JOHN MACLAUCHLAN, Chief Librarian and Curator of
the Dundee Free Library and Museum, . . 39

WM. ARCHER, F.R.S., M.R.I.A., Librarian of the
National Library of Ireland, ... 41

J. T. CLARK, Keeper of the Advocates' Library,
Edinburgh, ... 43

F. T. BARRETT, Librarian of the Mitchell Library,
Glasgow, ... 45

JOHN D. MULLINS, Librarian of the Free Libraries,
Birmingham, ... 47

Rev. S. D. F. SALMOND, M.A., D.D., Professor of
Systematic Theology in the Free Church College,
Aberdeen, ... 49 .

Rev. A. M. FAIRBAIRN, D.D., Principal of Airedale
College, . . . : 51

EXPRESSIONS OF OPINION with respect to the Anderson Free
Library Catalogue from—

J. T. CLARK, Librarian, Edinburgh, ... 53

JOHN MACLAUCHLAN, Librarian, Dundee, . . . 53

F. T. BARRETT, Librarian, Glasgow, ... 54

CHAS. R. BALLARD, Librarian, Ames Free Library,
Massachusetts, U.S.A., ... 54

Rev. J. CLARE HUDSON, Horncastle, ... 54

The Late Professor STANLEY JEVONS, . . . 55

"THE ABERDEEN DAILY FREE PRESS," . . . 55

"THE ACADEMY," 55

To The

PUBLIC LIBRARY COMMITTEE

OF THE

Burgh of Aberdeen.

My Lord Provost and Gentlemen,

I beg leave respectfully to offer myself for the office of Librarian, and to submit for your consideration the following statement and testimony.

I am 37 years of age, a Graduate of the University here, having taken the degree of M.A., with Honours in Classics, in 1866, and a Life Member of the Library Association of the United Kingdom.

Having had my attention early directed to the growth of Free Public Libraries, both in this country and in the United States of America, and been led to recognise the important function they are destined to fulfil in relation to the work of popular education, I have for several years looked forward to attaining the position of acting head of such an institution, and have assiduously endeavoured to qualify myself professionally for it.

With this view, in addition to the further prosecution of my University studies, I have given myself a general training in Modern Languages (French,

German and Italian), in Bibliography, and in other branches bearing upon the duties of a Librarian. At the same time, I have made myself thoroughly conversant with the management of Free Libraries at home and abroad, and have studied on the spot the working of several of the most successful organisations in this country.

In 1875, I arranged and catalogued the valuable Library, numbering about 5000 volumes, belonging to Sir William Forbes, Bart. of Craigievar. In 1880-1, I was entrusted by Sir John Anderson with the work of organising and preparing a printed catalogue for the Anderson Free Library, Woodside (a copy of which is herewith submitted); and, in 1881-2, I was engaged by the Right Hon. the Earl of Fife to select, arrange and catalogue his very fine Library at Duff House, numbering about 15,000 volumes, representing almost every leading class of literature, ancient and modern, English and foreign.

For the past five years, I have held the post of Assistant-Librarian in the University of Aberdeen. In that capacity, I have had under my charge the entire Medical and Law sections of its Library, together with two subsidiary collections of General Literature, embracing in all upwards of 25,000 volumes, and daily receiving fresh additions.

Born and bred in Aberdeen, I am naturally well acquainted with its special circumstances and requirements as a seat of industry and learning, and I should esteem it a privilege to be called to the duty of labouring to secure for my native city a Public Library worthy of its fame and adequate to its growing wants. My whole energy would be devoted to the work.

I have the honour to be,

MY LORD PROVOST AND GENTLEMEN,

Your obedient servant,

A. W. ROBERTSON.

THE UNIVERSITY,
ABERDEEN, *16th September, 1884.*

TESTIMONIALS.

From JOHN WEBSTER, LL.D., *Member of Parliament for the City of Aberdeen.*

EDGEHILL, ABERDEEN,
24th April, 1884.

I UNDERSTAND from my friend Mr. A. W. ROBERTSON, M.A., Librarian in Marischal College Library, that he intends to offer himself as a candidate for the office of Librarian of the Free Public Library of Aberdeen.

My long acquaintance with Mr. Robertson entitles me to offer an opinion of his fitness for such an office, for which I should hold him eminently qualified. He has had an admirable training in Literature, both in Classics and in English, and in Modern Continental Languages. Above all, he has made the work of a Librarian his special study for years, and is thoroughly versed in all its business of selecting, arranging and cataloguing large libraries. I was much gratified by the great skill displayed by him in his excellent catalogue of Sir John Anderson's Public Library at Woodside, wherein full information of the works it contains is afforded, and, above all, easy reference to every book which a reader may wish to consult.

I have pleasure in adding my testimony to Mr. Robertson's high personal character and to his pleasant and gentlemanly manners.

JOHN WEBSTER.

From SIR WILLIAM FORBES, Bart., *of Craigievar.*

FINTRAY HOUSE, ABERDEEN.

UNDERSTANDING that Mr. A. W. ROBERTSON, M.A., is to be a candidate for the office of Librarian of the Free Public Library in Aberdeen, I have very great pleasure in testifying, from my own personal knowledge and experience, to his character, abilities and marked fitness for so important and influential a position. For a period of about six months in 1875, Mr. Robertson was engaged by me in reorganising and recataloguing the Library here, consisting of some 5000 volumes, and during that time I formed a very high estimate of his character, being zealous, modest and unassuming. His scholarly attainments and qualifications as a Librarian, moreover, came out very clearly during the progress of the work, as it required an extensive and varied knowledge of books to be able to select from the very large number of volumes committed to his charge what should be retained and what laid aside. And I can most distinctly bear witness to the extremely careful manner in which he did the difficult work entrusted to him. Some of my friends, too, including the Librarian of one of the largest Libraries in the country, who have seen the Library as freshly arranged and the Catalogue prepared by Mr. Robertson, consider I was most fortunate in securing his services. Indeed the catalogue alone is sufficient to show at a glance that the compiler was thoroughly equal to the work he had undertaken. I most cordially recommend Mr. Robertson to the Public Library Committee.

WILLIAM FORBES, Bart.

From SIR JOHN ANDERSON, LL.D.

FAIRLEIGH, ST. LEONARDS-ON-SEA,
1*st May*, 1884.

A. W. ROBERTSON, Esq., M.A.
MY DEAR SIR,

In compliance with your request, I have much pleasure in bearing my testimony to the valuable services which you rendered in organizing the Library in the Public School at Woodside in 1881. The work was carried out under difficult conditions, still the Catalogue which you prepared is the best evidence of the value of your labour and of your intimate knowledge of books and systems of arrangement. A perusal of the Catalogue, which so far as I have heard has met with general approval, will bear out what I say more forcibly than any words of mine upon the subject.

Wishing you every prosperity in the pursuit of your delightful profession, and with kind regards,

I am,

Yours ever sincerely,

JOHN ANDERSON.

From JOHN F. WHITE, M.A., *Merchant in Aberdeen, and
Assessor in the University Court for the General Council
of the University of Aberdeen.*

ABERDEEN, 30*th August,* 1884.

I HAVE much pleasure in giving my opinion as to the
fitness of Mr. A. W. ROBERTSON, M.A., for the office
of Librarian of the Free Public Library of Aberdeen.

Mr. Robertson has many qualifications for the post.
His training in our University and his acquaintance
with modern languages are greatly in his favour,
while the experience he has gained as Librarian
at Marischal College and in other library work done
by him, has been very useful to him in connexion
with the profession which he has adopted. Knowing
Mr. Robertson's capacity for business and his zeal in
every work he undertakes, I feel sure that, if elected,
he will discharge the duties of the office with efficiency, and that his knowledge of our circumstances
and wants will be found of special use in the founda-
tion and management of our Public Library.

JOHN F. WHITE.

From WM. D. GEDDES, M.A., LL.D., *Professor of Greek in the University of Aberdeen.*

UNIVERSITY OF ABERDEEN,
30*th Aug.*, 1884.

HAVING been asked to express my opinion of the claims and qualifications of Mr. A. W. ROBERTSON, M.A., now a candidate for the office of Librarian of the Free Public Library for Aberdeen, I beg to testify as follows :

Mr. Robertson, who is a distinguished Graduate of the University, has now officiated for several years as Librarian at Marischal College, and in that capacity has had practically the management of a large and important section of the University Library. During this period he has uniformly given the highest satisfaction, and the Senatus has in consequence accorded to him a special advance of salary because of the value attached to his services. He possesses a great knowledge of Bibliography, has acquired extensive and varied experience in all the functions of a Librarian, and accordingly appears to me admirably adapted to fill the position to which he aspires. I may further add that I have recently had special opportunity to judge of his fitness from the experience I had of his excellent services in connexion with a small collection of antiquities, of which I happen to be in charge, and I found him most obliging and painstaking as well as trustworthy in all the duties he undertakes.

WM. D. GEDDES.

From Rev. WM. MILLIGAN, M.A., D.D., *Professor of Divinity and Biblical Criticism in the University of Aberdeen.*

THE UNIVERSITY, ABERDEEN,
8th Sept., 1884.

As I believe that the present Library of the Mechanics' Institution in this city is to be transferred to the Free Public Library about to be formed, I should not wish this testimonial to be used against the present respected Librarian of the Mechanics' Library. But on the supposition, either that that gentleman is not to be a candidate for the vacant post, or that the Committee of Management think it is desirable that a new and younger man should be placed at the head of the new Institution, I am free to speak.

In doing so, it is a great pleasure to me to think that I can in the most cordial and unhesitating manner bear witness to the high attainments and peculiar aptitudes which point to Mr. A. W. ROBERTSON as the man in every way fitted for the situation about to be filled up. I have long known Mr. Robertson. I have worked with him in the same office. I have had constant opportunities of knowing how he discharges his duties as Librarian at Marischal College, and he has always left but one impression upon my mind—that of his admirable fitness to be the Librarian of a great Public Library. He is naturally possessed of excellent abilities. He has been carefully educated, and the records of his College course show how he profited by his education. He has thorough literary tastes ; and he has devoted himself to the care of books as if it were the business of his life.

His experience in the management of a Library, and in the arranging and classifying and cataloguing of books, which is so extremely difficult a task, is such as has fallen to very few men of his age ; and he has always given the greatest satisfaction to his employers in his present position. He is of active habits and obliging disposition, and his whole demeanour is always that of a gentleman. Besides this, no man knows better the wants of the working men of Aberdeen, and his advice as to the purchasing of books will be most valuable. I can recommend him with great confidence to the Committee. They will not easily get one, as I believe, in all respects so well qualified and so worthy of their choice.

WM. MILLIGAN, D.D.,
Professor of Divinity and Biblical Criticism.

From Rev. JOHN FYFE, M.A., *Professor of Moral Philosophy in the University of Aberdeen, and Curator of the University Library.*

UNIVERSITY OF ABERDEEN,
10*th Sept.*, 1884.

I AM convinced that ALEXANDER W. ROBERTSON, M.A., is highly qualified for the office of Keeper of the Free Public Library of Aberdeen : because he has taken full advantage of the general mental culture afforded by a University education ; because he has an enthusiasm for library work ; because he has had considerable experience in the various departments of library work, and has been successful in all ; because he is naturally active and will spare no exertion ; and because whilst straightforward and firm he is very pleasant and obliging.

As a citizen of Aberdeen I should be delighted to hear that he had been appointed Librarian, so that the Institution might have a favourable start.

JOHN FYFE.

From WM. STIRLING, M.D., Sc.D., *Professor of Institutes of Medicine in the University of Aberdeen.*

THE UNIVERSITY OF ABERDEEN,
2nd September, 1884.

IT is with the most perfect confidence that I venture to recommend to the Committee of Management of the Free Public Library in Aberdeen Mr. A. W. ROBERTSON, M.A., as a gentleman in every way specially well qualified to fill the post of Librarian of our Free Public Library.

For several years I have come into direct and, I may say, almost daily contact with Mr. Robertson in the course of his official duties as Librarian in Marischal College, and I can confidently state that he is a trained, experienced and cultured Librarian of the highest stamp. Mr. Robertson is a most excellent business man, punctual, accurate and thoroughly reliable, and he is invariably most courteous and obliging. Not only is Mr. Robertson an accomplished scholar, but he has a specially wide knowledge of several modern languages. Moreover he is, from long experience and training, thoroughly acquainted with the special circumstances and requirements of the district, a point of great moment in the construction of a Public Library.

In writing a testimonial, it is difficult for me to say all that I should like to say as to Mr. Robertson's most admirable qualities, but I may sum up my opinion by stating that Mr. Robertson is in every respect a perfect type of what a Librarian ought to be, and I am perfectly satisfied that if he be appointed to the post he will make our Public Library a complete success.

WM. STIRLING, M.D., Sc.D.

From JAMES W. H. TRAIL, M.A., M.D., *Professor of Botany in the University of Aberdeen.*

MONTREAL, CANADA,
3rd Sept., 1884.

MR. ROBERTSON having asked me to express my opinion of his qualifications for the position of Librarian of the proposed Free Public Library in Aberdeen, I have the greatest pleasure and confidence in stating my belief that he is exceptionally well fitted in every way for the office. For several years, Mr. Robertson has been in charge of the University Library in Marischal College Buildings in Aberdeen, and in that capacity he has shown the utmost care and skill, and discharged the duties of his position very efficiently in every way. In the course of the past year he has given much labour to the preparation of a Subject-catalogue of the books in the Library on a novel and ingenious plan of his own.

Mr. Robertson has also been engaged in the arrangement of other libraries both public and private in the North of Scotland, and having made it a special aim to acquaint himself with the condition and circumstances of the district, he is peculiarly fitted for the charge of a large Public Library in Aberdeen. During a long and intimate intercourse with Mr. Robertson, in which the management of Public Libraries was a frequent theme of discussion, I have always admired his wide knowledge of books and familiarity with the best methods of dealing with them in the public interest.

For these reasons I believe that it would be greatly to the advantage of the proposed Public Library were Mr. Robertson placed in charge of it, though I should regret the loss to the University were he to be removed, as he would thereby be, from the service of the University of Aberdeen.

JAMES W. H. TRAIL, M.A., M.D.,
Professor of Botany in the University of Aberdeen.

From ALEX. DYCE DAVIDSON, M.A., M.D., *Professor of Materia Medica in the University of Aberdeen.*

224 UNION STREET, ABERDEEN,
16*th Sept.*, 1884.

I HAVE known Mr. A. W. ROBERTSON, M.A., intimately during the last five years, and judging by his knowledge of the duties of a Librarian and his helpful obliging manner, I believe that he is in every way well qualified for the office of Librarian of the Free Public Library of Aberdeen. With one at its head such as he is—cultured, energetic and enthusiastic in his work, it cannot fail to make a fair start and ultimately attain high success.

ALEX. DYCE DAVIDSON.

From W. MINTO, M.A., *Professor of Logic and English Language and Literature in the University of Aberdeen.*

UNIVERSITY OF ABERDEEN,
15th Sept., 1884.

UNDERSTANDING that Mr. A. W. ROBERTSON, M.A., is a candidate for the office of Librarian of the Aberdeen Free Library, I have much pleasure in testifying in the strongest manner, and from personal knowledge, to his eminent qualifications for the post.

Mr. Robertson has all his life been a student of wide range, and the diversity of his knowledge of books is one great element of fitness. He has had experience as a Librarian in the Marischal College Library, and has there shown unfailing courtesy and an obliging readiness to put his wide and accurate knowledge at the service of readers. But besides this, Mr. Robertson has had exceptional experience in the arrangement and cataloguing of several large collections of books, and in this work has shown not only clearness of method and an acquaintance with library arrangement as practised elsewhere, but inventive originality in the contrivance of the means of convenient reference. The classification of books is an extremely difficult problem, and Mr. Robertson has solved it more than once with great judgment.

As far as regards Bibliography, and knowledge of where books are to be had and the prices to be paid for them, I believe Mr. Robertson has few equals. And bearing in mind also the honourable connexion of his family with Aberdeen, I have no hesitation in saying that in my belief his qualifications for the office that he solicits are unique. Apart from any local connexion, there are few if any more accomplished librarians to be found in the kingdom.

W. MINTO.

From ALEX. OGSTON, M.A., M.D., *Professor of Surgery in the University of Aberdeen.*

252 UNION STREET, ABERDEEN,
6th September, 1884.

DEAR MR. ROBERTSON,

I do not think it likely that so suitable a Curator of the Free Public Library in Aberdeen as yourself will be easily found, and therefore gladly testify as to what I know of your capabilities.

During the last five years in which you have had charge of the Libraries in Marischal College, the department there has been conducted in a way that has given every satisfaction. Order and efficiency have been everywhere, and any difficulty or inquiry has always been met in the most courteous and harmonious spirit.

I have not failed to perceive that your knowledge of books is an extensive one, and that your skill as a linguist is such as becomes the head of a large library; and I should add that, so far as I am able to judge, your views regarding the mutual co-operation and assistance of libraries in general, a very important matter indeed for one aiming at the post you seek, are in accordance with those of the wisest and most cultured of our day.

It is further evident that your University training as a graduate, and your local knowledge as an Aberdonian must, when conjoined with your other qualifications, be of much value in connexion with our Free Public Library.

Believing as I do that your character and disposition are all that can be desired in one whose main aim must be to develop the usefulness of such an institution, I shall, should you be appointed to the office of Librarian, rejoice that our Free Library has found a worthy head.

I am, DEAR MR. ROBERTSON,

Yours truly,

ALEX. OGSTON.

A. W. ROBERTSON, Esq., M.A.

From ROBERT WALKER, M.A., F.R.S.E., *Librarian to the University of Aberdeen.*

UNIVERSITY LIBRARY, ABERDEEN,
10*th September*, 1884.

I HAVE much pleasure in expressing the opinion that Mr. A. W. ROBERTSON, A.M., who at present assists me in the charge of the New Town Section of this Library, is thoroughly well qualified for the superintendence of the Free Public Library of this city.

When, five years ago, he offered himself for the office which he now holds in this Library, I felt that the University was very fortunate in being able to secure the services of one of our Graduates in Honours, who had already given special attention to library work, and had done a great deal in arranging and cataloguing large collections.

The very varied experience which Mr. Robertson has since then acquired in the actual working of this Library seems to me to have supplied precisely that element in his training for the charge of a large library which might be considered lacking in his previous career. His duties here have been much beyond routine. The accessions to the New Town portion of the Library have during his time been very extensive, including a very large number of foreign works, and every work added has passed through Mr. Robertson's hands at almost every stage until its final absorption into the collection. In revising Mr. Robertson's titling of newly-added books (a work which in the first instance I have been in the habit of leaving to himself), I have not only had occasion to note his great accuracy, but I have profited by the judgment and acuteness of his remarks when any question of special intricacy turned up for our consideration.

Mr. Robertson has lately been engaged on a Subject-catalogue of the collection, which will prove of great advantage to Specialists in all departments. Not only has the whole of this work been of his own execution, but the plan also is, in some features, of his own devising.

In all his work Mr. Robertson has given entire satisfaction. At the end of each Library-year the report sent to the Senatus has been of a highly satisfactory character: on more than one occasion *not one single volume having gone amissing* during the previous twelvemonth.

Mr. Robertson's courteous and obliging manner has often been made the subject of remark to me by Library readers, and I can truly say that, should he be appointed Librarian of the Free Public Library of Aberdeen, we shall greatly regret the loss of his valuable services.

I leave it to others to speak of Mr. Robertson's extensive knowledge of books and of his special fitness from education, taste, and other qualifications for the charge of our Free Public Library. I can, however, with confidence, and I do with much pleasure, testify what I have seen of the ability, efficiency and faithfulness of all his work here.

It will not, in my judgment, be easy to find one who possesses equally high claims to the office.

ROBERT WALKER,
Librarian.

From RICHARD GARNETT, LL.D., *Superintendent of the Reading Room of the British Museum.*

BRITISH MUSEUM, 11*th Sept.,* 1884.

GENTLEMEN,

I have great pleasure in bearing testimony to the qualifications of Mr. A. W. ROBERTSON, who is a candidate for the office of Librarian of the Free Public Library of Aberdeen. Having been frequently in communication with Mr. Robertson, I can speak of his abilities, and also of the intimate knowledge and experience which he possesses of the duties of a Librarian. Such preliminary experience added to his academic training would, in my opinion, be an indispensable requisite for the management of a Library like yours ; and the fact that it is to a great extent a special local experience of the needs and requirements of your own city must greatly enhance its value.

I remain, GENTLEMEN,

With great respect,

Your obedient servant,

RICHARD GARNETT,
Superintendent Reading Room, British Museum.

TO THE
PUBLIC LIBRARY COMMITTEE,
ABERDEEN.

From JOHN MACLAUCHLAN, *Chief Librarian and Curator of
the Dundee Free Library and Museum.*

FREE LIBRARY, MUSEUM AND FINE ART GALLERY,
ALBERT INSTITUTE,
DUNDEE, 28*th April*, 1884.

I KNOW of no person who unites in himself in so high
a degree all the essential qualities necessary to consti-
tute a good and efficient Librarian as Mr. A. W.
ROBERTSON, M.A.

He has love for the office, having, with many other
eligible spheres of labour open to him, deliberately
chosen the profession of Librarian, and thus he discharges the duties which fall to that situation with
that enthusiasm which, possessing as he does the
other requisite qualities, insures success.

He has had the advantage of a regular academical
education which I consider of the highest importance,
if not indispensable, in any one aspiring to become
the managing head of a Public Library in Aberdeen.

He has also had a very wide and varied experience
in Library work. Of one important branch of that
work, namely, that of cataloguing, I have made a
close and careful examination, and have found it to
be executed with great intelligence and the utmost
accuracy. Mr. Robertson thoroughly understands

the vexed question of cataloguing, which of recent years has been much discussed by the Society of Arts and the Library Association of the United Kingdom, and is now settled on principles clearly understood by Mr. Robertson.

In view of all the circumstances, I consider that the Aberdeen Public Library Committee are exceptionally fortunate in having in their city one so competent to organise and to manage their Institution, and one moreover possessed of what an outsider could not possibly have—but what is always of great value —an intimate knowledge of the special tastes and wants of Aberdeen.

I have very great pleasure in recommending him to the Committee.

JOHN MACLAUCHLAN,
Chief Librarian and Curator, Dundee Free
Library and Museum.

From WM. ARCHER, F.R.S., M.R.I.A., *Librarian of the National Library of Ireland.*

NATIONAL LIBRARY OF IRELAND,
SCIENCE AND ART DEPARTMENT, LEINSTER HOUSE,
KILDARE STREET, DUBLIN, 11*th Sept.*, 1884.

IT affords me great pleasure to bear my testimony to the high qualifications and fitness of Mr. A. W. ROBERTSON, M.A., for the Librarianship of the Free Public Library of the City of Aberdeen.

In paying a number of visits to different libraries in various parts of the country in order myself to profit by the hints and experience to be thus acquired, I had the pleasure to call at the Marischal College amongst others, and thus I had a somewhat prolonged opportunity and to me the great advantage to converse with Mr. Robertson on various subjects connected with library administration and economy. It was very plain that he had his heart in his work, and from his experience and knowledge I derived many valuable ideas. Although Mr. Robertson is placed in a library different in purpose and tone from that about to be established, he has had great experience collaterally in the work of a library of more popular character, and of this his " Anderson Free Library Catalogue " stands as abundant evidence. He has in fact a many-sided experience in that and in private libraries which gives him all the greater claim.

I know that much more which would be completely justified might be said in favour of Mr. Robertson, which would however be superfluous to dwell upon as regards one so well known in his native city. I shall only say that I know Mr. Robertson has thoroughly devoted himself to the work of a Librarian, and feel satisfied he would throw his heart into the duties— and this latter is " half the battle ".

Having already borne deserved evidence in favour of another candidate, I may, I trust, be permitted to add that I consider this to be in itself quite justifiable, both being, I feel assured, thoroughly fit men ; and I hope I may say, without being thought too bold, that the Committee is to be congratulated in having at least two so highly eligible candidates for selection. But it is indeed not without much diffidence that I venture to come forward at all to call attention to the qualifications of another, so capable as Mr. Robertson of teaching myself in so many things. But still I think, when I have a good opportunity, I can discern a man of capacity.

It is then but simple justice to come forward as I am now doing and bear evidence to the simple truth as regards Mr. Robertson's thorough fitness for the post for which he is a candidate.

WM. ARCHER, F.R.S., M.R.I.A.,
Librarian.

From J. T. CLARK, *Keeper of the Advocates' Library,*
Edinburgh.

I HAVE much pleasure in testifying to Mr. A. W.
ROBERTSON's qualifications as a Librarian.

From my knowledge of his extensive and varied
experience and attainments, and of the way in which
he can do general library work, as well as cataloguing,
as evidenced in his " Catalogue of the Anderson Free
Library " and in the Catalogue of the Library at
Fintray House, I believe him well qualified to fill the
post to which he now aspires.

J. T. CLARK.

From F. T. BARRETT, *Librarian of the Mitchell Library, Glasgow.*

ALTHOUGH I have not the advantage of a personal acquaintance with Mr. A. W. ROBERTSON, M.A., of Aberdeen University, it gives me pleasure to state that I have had an opportunity of examining the Catalogue of the Anderson Free Library at Woodside, compiled by him, and have had some correspondence with him on matters relating to library work.

The catalogue before-mentioned is, in my opinion, a well-thought-out and carefully executed piece of work ; and Mr. Robertson's letters further indicate a thorough study of and acquaintance with that important department of the duties of an acting Librarian.

F. T. BARRETT.

From JOHN D. MULLINS, *Chief Librarian, Free Libraries, Birmingham.*

BIRMINGHAM CENTRAL FREE LIBRARY,
4th September, 1884.

DEAR SIR,

I am sorry that I did not see you while you were here.

Pray accept thanks for your excellent catalogue of the Anderson Free Library.

I should think from your application that your chance of success in your present candidature must be very considerable, you having the combined advantages of high educational acquirements, experience of library work, and local knowledge.

Yours respectfully,
JOHN D. MULLINS.

A. W. ROBERTSON, Esq., M.A.,
University Library, Aberdeen.

From Rev. S. D. F. SALMOND, M.A., D.D., *Professor of Systematic Theology in the Free Church College, Aberdeen.*

FREE CHURCH COLLEGE, ABERDEEN,
6th September, 1884.

MY acquaintance with Mr. A. W. ROBERTSON dates from his student days, and has given me abundant opportunities of recognising his capabilities in various lines. I have pleasure, therefore, in expressing the opinion that he possesses very high qualifications for such a post as that of Librarian in a great Public Institution. His scholarship is undoubted and embraces familiarity not only with the classical languages, but also with several of the modern languages most necessary in the position referred to. He has given himself to the Librarian's work as the task of his life, and has sought every opportunity of qualifying himself as an expert in it. He has done much excellent work in the selection and arrangement of several Libraries of importance, and has commended himself to those who have had to deal with him in his present situation by his unfailing urbanity and attentiveness. Being at the same time a native of the city, acquainted with its special circumstances and requirements, having received his own Academic training in its University, and having intimate knowledge of its educational needs and interests, he seems to be uncommonly well furnished for the position of acting head of the officials who shall be put in charge of the Free Public Library of Aberdeen.

S. D. F. SALMOND, D.D.,
Professor of Theology.

·

From Rev. A. M. FAIRBAIRN, D.D., *Principal of Airedale College.* *

ABERDEEN, 8*th Jan.*, 1877.

I HAVE learned with much pleasure that Mr. A. W. ROBERTSON, M.A., is a candidate for the office of Librarian of the University Library of Aberdeen. I have known Mr. Robertson for several years, have had many opportunities of judging as to his personal tastes and aptitudes, and now wish to express the conviction that he is in a high degree qualified for the above office. Of his practical capacity in arranging and managing a Library others can speak, but I can testify that he has for years applied himself to Librarianship as his life's profession, and that this predilection has induced him to undertake preparatory work of various kinds, especially the study of Bibliography and the more important Modern Languages.

Mr. Robertson has an excellent literary taste, and has proved himself possessed of good critical ability. He is well qualified to form a judgment of the intrinsic merits of a book, and also to inform himself as to the

---

* Owing to Dr. Fairbairn's absence from this country it has not been possible to communicate with him on the subject of the present candidature.

commercial questions connected with it. I am certain that the Library Committee would find him a thoroughly intelligent and sympathetic collaborator, well informed as to the state of the book market, both old and new, home and foreign.

Mr. Robertson is of a most obliging disposition, quiet and unassuming spirit, punctual and systematic in his habits, kind yet firm in manner.

For the above reasons I have every confidence in expressing my belief in Mr. Robertson's eminent fitness for the office he seeks, and I wish him every success in his candidature.

A. M. FAIRBAIRN.

OPINIONS OF LIBRARIANS AND OTHERS WITH RESPECT TO THE CATALOGUE OF THE ANDERSON FREE LIBRARY, WOODSIDE.

I HAVE examined portions of the Anderson Free Library Catalogue very carefully as well as the plan on which it is drawn up, and have come to the conclusion that, besides giving a great deal of well-compacted information, it will prove as completely suitable for the requirements of the readers of the Woodside Library as any catalogue could be. I found it freer from small errors than any catalogue I know, and that is no small compliment to its careful compilation.

J. T. CLARK,
Keeper of the Advocates' Library, Edinburgh.

I HAVE great pleasure in congratulating you on the Catalogue, which is constructed on *the plan* of which I approve, and is done in a manner reflecting great credit on you. It is a very handsome, well-printed volume, fulfilling the first and most essential condition of being easily consulted. I do not think there need be further discussion as to the supreme merit of the Dictionary Catalogue—that I think has now passed into the safe region of settled questions. Of course the best system will fail, if not properly carried out, but yours is safe on that score. I like above all things your Preface—admire the clear, terse and decided way in which you explain your system.

JOHN MACLAUCHLAN,
Librarian, Free Public Library, Dundee.

———

Few indeed of the Free Libraries in the provinces are enabled to give their readers so ample an index to their contents as is furnished by the Catalogue of the Anderson Free Library. It is very thoroughly done.

F. T. BARRETT,
Librarian, Mitchell Library, Glasgow.

———

I HAVE examined with much satisfaction a copy of the Catalogue of the Anderson Free Library, compiled by A. W. ROBERTSON, M.A. It is a first-rate piece of work, admirably conceived and as admirably executed. It compares, in my opinion, very favourably with the catalogues of similar institutions in this country, some forty in number, that have come under my notice.

CHARLES R. BALLARD,
Librarian, Ames Free Library, North Easton,
Massachusetts, U.S.A.

———

HAVING carefully examined the excellent Catalogue of the Anderson Free Library, I have much pleasure in recording my high opinion of its merits. The ar-

rangement is well conceived and admirably carried
out. In particular, I am much pleased with the
rather novel feature of the Short-Title classed catalogue appended to it.

REV. J. CLARE HUDSON,
Librarian, Mechanics' Institution, Horncastle.

I WAS much pleased to receive a copy of the Catalogue
of the Anderson Free Library. I have carefully
looked over it and have formed a high opinion of its
plan and execution.

THE LATE PROFESSOR STANLEY JEVONS.

THE Catalogue of the Anderson Free Library is worthy
of notice as probably the first thoroughly prepared
library catalogue with which the public in the North
of Scotland have had the opportunity of becoming
acquainted ; and as such it reflects very high credit
upon its compiler, Mr. A. W. ROBERTSON, M.A. The
different headings in the main part of the catalogue
follow strict alphabetical order in the Dictionary form;
and the numbers prefixed give at once the class to
which the book belongs, and the division, with the
precise place it occupies therein.

Aberdeen Daily Free Press, 9th Aug., 1881.

THE Free Library presented by Sir John Anderson
to his native town of Woodside, near Aberdeen, was
opened on August 13th. Its value for use is much

enhanced by the *Catalogue*.   This we have before us, and can testify to its elaborate and workman-like character.   The titles of the books are printed at full length, and in not a few cases the contents are analysed.   At the end is added a short-titled list of the contents of the library as they stand classified on the shelves.

The Academy, 20th Aug., 1881.

ABERDEEN UNIVERSITY PRESS.

FREE PUBLIC LIBRARY OF ABERDEEN.

THE UNIVERSITY LIBRARY, MARISCHAL COLLEGE,

ABERDEEN, *April 22nd*, 1884.

MY LORD PROVOST AND GENTLEMEN,

Presuming that you will presently be requiring the services of a Librarian for the Free Public Library, I beg leave respectfully to lay before you a brief statement of my qualifications for the post.

I am a Graduate of the University here, having taken the degree of M.A., with Honours in Classics, in 1866, and am also a Life Member of the Library Association of the United Kingdom.

Having had my attention early directed to the growth of Free Public Libraries both in this country and in the United States of America, and been led to recognise the important function they are destined to fulfil in relation to the great work of popular education, I have for several years aspired to the position of Acting Head of the Staff of such an Institution, and have assiduously endeavoured to qualify myself professionally as a Librarian.

In this connection I may mention that, in addition to the further prosecution of my

Librarian. At the same time, I have made myself thoroughly conversant with the best methods of conducting Free Libraries, as practised in several of the large towns of this country and of America. During the course of several years' experience of the actual work of a Librarian I have acquired a considerable knowledge of the tastes and requirements of the public in the matter of books. As bearing upon this, I may add that, in 1875, I arranged and catalogued the valuable Library, numbering about 5000 volumes, belonging to Sir William Forbes, Bart., of Craigievar; in 1880-81 I was entrusted with the work of organising and preparing a printed Catalogue for the Anderson Free Library, Woodside; and in 1881-82 I was engaged by the Right Hon. the Earl of Fife to select, arrange, and catalogue his very fine Library at Duff House, numbering about 15,000 volumes, representing almost every leading class of literature, ancient and modern, English and foreign.

For the past five years I have been acting as Assistant-Librarian in the University here. In that capacity I have had under my charge the entire Medical and Law section of its Library, together with two subsidiary collections of general literature, embracing in all upwards of 25,000 volumes, and daily receiving fresh additions, native and foreign.

Meanwhile, I desire only further to say that at the proper time I shall be prepared to submit to you for your consideration a number of testimonials, some of them from eminent Librarians, which will certify to the character of the work I have accomplished, and to my general fitness for the important post to which I now aspire.

I have the honour to be,

My Lord Provost and Gentlemen,

Your obedient Servant,

A. W. ROBERTSON.

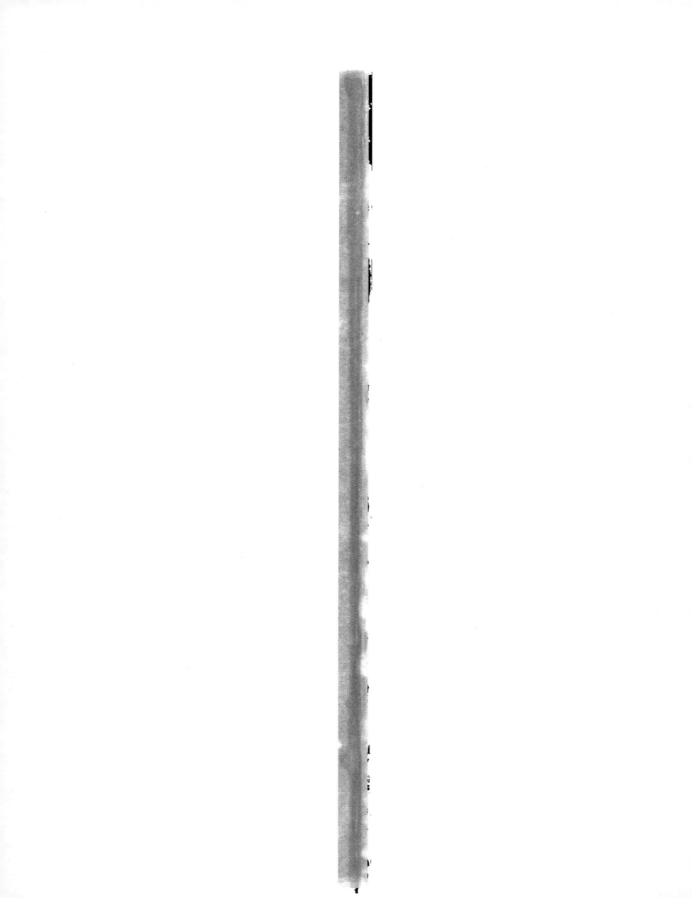